JANET SCHAEFFLER, OP

Calming Meditations for *busy* Catechists

TWENTY-THIRD PUBLICATIONS
twentythirdpublications.com

Twenty-Third Publications
977 Hartford Turnpike Unit A
Waterford, CT 06385
(860) 437-3012 or (800) 321-0411
twentythirdpublications.com

Second Printing 2023

Cover photo: ©maram/stock.adobe.com

ISBN: 978-1-62785-696-6
Printed in the U.S.A.

bayard A Division of Bayard, Inc.

Contents

When I'm Planning a Session

Planning takes time; it might feel redundant and monotonous. Yet, one of Benjamin Franklin's wise sayings was: "If you fail to plan, you are planning to fail!" Because of the responsibility of catechizing, planning is vital—and is God's work.

To make your planning time energetic, creative, and faith-filled, surround yourself with many ideas related to the session's theme: your text, a list of resources from the parish, your gathering file (see the action below), your family, happenings in your school/parish, neighborhood, world, and what others who are teaching the same session are doing.

Give yourself as much time as possible to ponder and pray. With time for quiet, choose from all your thoughts and resources, writing a session plan that includes the session's key elements in your text.

CALMING MEDITATION ■ As you sit down to plan your session, place your hands on the arm of your chair. Imagine that the arms of your chair are the arms of God supporting and holding you. As you plan your catechetical session, know that you, your learners, and your plans are held in God's hands.

COMMITTED ACTION ■ Create a gathering file: Make a file folder for each of the themes/topics your text covers. When you see/hear a poem, a song, a prayer, a current event, etc., that relates to a theme, file it away so that when you come to plan each session, you will have a plethora of ideas to choose from.

When I Don't Know the Families of My Learners

Faith does not grow in isolation; the faith of each one of us (especially children and youth) is impacted by all we are, all we do, and all the people in our lives. For young people, the most constant and enduring influence is their parents and families.

Be creative and intentional in getting to know the parents and families of your children and youth. Knowing them, having a relationship with them, will help you design your sessions and the examples you use. The families and children will be touched by the personal interest you show in them.

Before the year begins, call the parents to introduce yourself. Ask what you can do for them; ask for their ideas on how you can work alongside them as together you surround their child with a faith-filled environment. Respond to the families throughout the year, especially to any happenings you hear about: births, illness, special achievements, deaths.

CALMING MEDITATION ■ *God of All Families, bless the families with whom and to whom I will be ministering during this year. As you protect and care for them, empower me to be a faith-filled witness, a sign of your love for them.*

COMMITTED ACTION ■ Make a plan to call or email each parent (perhaps one family each week) to give a compliment about their child, sharing something considerate they have done or a trait/virtue you have witnessed in them.

When I Don't Feel Creative

What do we mean by creativity? Our role is not to be an art teacher. When we do use artistic expression—and we should—it's for the purpose of helping others delve deeper into meanings and express for themselves their understanding of the connection between faith and life.

God made us human, gifting us with creativity. All people have the capacity to be creative.

Steve Jobs said, "Creativity is just connecting things. When you ask creative people how they did something, they feel a little guilty because they didn't really do it, they just saw something. It seemed obvious to them after a while. That's because they were able to connect experiences they've had and synthesize new things." That's what catechists do: connect faith and everyday life.

Creativity in our learning times can be invited and enhanced as we create opportunities for reflection; go beyond textbooks and worksheets and work with a variety of learning materials; provide hands-on learning; encourage learners to choose the format they want to follow for their response (a photo essay, skit, diorama, video, or recipe); explore different cultures; and create an atmosphere of community building and cooperation.

CALMING MEDITATION ■ *God of Creativity, inspire me, guide me, in enthusiastically seeing with new eyes, connecting your love to all I'm called to do.*

COMMITTED ACTION ■ As you plan your sessions, ask: Do the activities allow for the imagination, the dreaming, the wondering, the response of each learner, or do I expect the end result to be the way I want it?

When Everything Seems to Be Changing

The Greek philosopher Heraclitus of Ephesus wrote (in more than 100 pieces of his writings), "Change is the only constant." Over the years, this saying has been revised to "The only constant in life is change."

All of us can say that we experience the constancy of change in countless ways today. As catechists, we, too, meet it in various ways: new ways of catechizing are suggested; the needs of children and families always seem to be multiplying; many parishes—and their organizational structures—are changing; parishes are being closed, clustered, or merged; and so on.

As committed catechists, respond to change through the 4 Ps: Patiently; Persistently (not giving up); Positively (with Christian hope); and staying rooted in Purpose (responding to God's call to serve).

CALMING MEDITATION ■ Throughout the ages, one form of meditation has been to silently repeat a sacred word (mantra) or Scripture passage. Choose a short passage from Scripture which you can pray often throughout the day, such as "*The Lord is my shepherd, I shall not want*" (Psalm 23:1); "*Do not let your hearts be troubled, and do not let them be afraid*" (John 14:27); "*Cast your burden on the Lord, and he will sustain you*" (Psalm 55:23); or "*I am with you always, to the end of the age*" (Matthew 28:20).

COMMITTED ACTION ■ When you are experiencing change in your catechetical setting or parish, write down the positives that are coming (or might come) from the change.

When I'm Not Experiencing What I'm Teaching

Do you ever feel: I'm teaching about a God of Comfort, but I often feel anxious and worried. I'm teaching about a God of Joy, but I'm experiencing disappointments and burdens. I'm teaching about a God of Unceasing Nearness, but at times I don't feel God is with me, especially in the hard times. I'm teaching about a God of Strength and Promise, but I feel as though I don't know where to turn, what to do next.

Living a faith-filled life doesn't mean there won't be setbacks or difficult times. Being a catechist doesn't mean that everything will be perfect, carefree, and peaceful in our lives. Perhaps it's because of our questions, our real-life experiences of uncertainties, concerns, and fears, that we can better understand our learners and their families, that we learn more and more to depend on the God who can always be trusted.

CALMING MEDITATION ■ *Reassuring God, deepen in me the peace that only you can give. Help me to always hear you say, "You don't have to know the way. I do."*

COMMITTED ACTION ■ As you prepare your sessions and lead your young people through them, through an exploration of our Compassionate God of Constant Presence, take time to pretend that you are the learner. What are you hearing in God's message? How and what does God want you to learn, to reflect on, to deepen at this time in your journey of life?

When My Heart Isn't in It

For many of us, we experience highs and lows, times of enthusiasm and times of sluggishness. At times we might not have the interest to prepare one more session, to show up eagerly one more week.

The amazing and comforting reality is that even when we feel our heart isn't in it, God's heart—and confidence—is always in us. As we are centered in God—even amid the low times—we continue to pray (Psalm 61:1–2), we continue to rely on others who have experienced what we are going through (Psalm 61:5); we continue to count our blessings (Psalm 61:8); we continue to stay faithful to our call (Psalm 61:8).

Our enthusiasm (from a Greek word meaning "full of God") is restored when we deepen our awareness that God is within us; God never abandons us, even on the lethargic days.

CALMING MEDITATION ■ *Faithful God, I am grateful for my gifts, even on the days when I feel I have nothing to give. I am grateful for your strength in me, especially when I feel I have no strength left. I am grateful for joy, even when everything seems gloomy. I am grateful for your call, especially when I know I can't do it alone.*

COMMITTED ACTION ■ In your journal, list three things that went right in your planning, in your sessions—even on the days your heart wasn't in it.

When My Learners Aren't in Church on Sunday

Often, we might hear from our young people, "We don't go to Mass on Sunday." This presents a challenging, precarious balance: to not respond in judgment, yet to share the importance of and gifts from celebrating the liturgy with the community weekly.

Of course, the decision to participate in Sunday liturgy is not often the child's; hence, we don't want to make them responsible for something that might be out of their control.

They might not be at the liturgy, but they are with us each week. Often it takes only one significant person to be an enthusiastic, faith-filled model—and nudger—in a child's life. Catechists can be that person. When we speak often of the privilege and joy of worshipping together, of God's invitation to the Table, of the comfort and challenge of Sunday liturgy, we are planting seeds. When we use liturgical rituals during our sessions (the Sign of Peace, the Sign of the Cross on our foreheads, lips, and heart before the Gospel) and link them to liturgy, we are planting seeds for participation.

CALMING MEDITATION ■ *Faithful God, you call us to worship as a community. Deepen that desire, that gift of unity in Eucharist, in each one of us.*

COMMITTED ACTION ■ Send an email to your learners' families, suggesting things to watch for in the coming weekend liturgy (a line from the readings, a General Intercession for the parish's First Communicants, etc.).

When There Doesn't Seem to Be Enough Time for Each Learner

Our time together in each of our catechetical sessions is so short, and each learner is unique, with their own gifts, personalities, questions, joys, and sorrows. Often it feels as though there is not enough time to respond to each child/youth individually and uniquely. Do they feel anonymous, just a nameless person within the group? Do they feel as though getting through the content is more important than their questions, thoughts, and experiences?

One catechist I know ends each session by prayerfully sharing the Sign of Peace with each learner as they leave their gathering space. This is one small but significant way to be sure she has spoken to each child individually and by name.

CALMING MEDITATION ■ *Visio divina* is similar to *lectio divina*; instead of Scripture, *visio divina* uses visual elements to help set your mind on prayer. It invites God to speak to your heart through the image. Often, we use icons and religious art, but any type of visual can be employed. During your personal prayer each week, choose a photo of one of your learners. As you pray for them, see their goodness. Imagine them wrapped in God's love, protection, and care.

COMMITTED ACTION ■ Each week, send one child a happy-gram, a note to compliment them, to let them know how glad you are to see them each week and to let them know of your prayer for them.

When I Don't Know Enough about This Week's Topic

Perhaps it would be true to say, "We never will." There will always be more to learn, more to appreciate, more to celebrate, and more to do. One of the gifts of being a catechist is that a journey of study and deepened understanding is inherent in what we do: as we prepare and as we listen to the insights of others—all those on the journey with us, especially the often provocative thoughts of the children and youth.

At the same time, there might be times we do feel that this week's topic is beyond us or confusing.

I recall observing my two-year-old great-nephew watching *Who Wants to Be a Millionaire?*. As soon as a question was asked, he delighted in responding, "Phone a friend," "Ask the audience," or "50-50."

We, too, have many lifelines. Rely on your parish catechetical leader, other catechists, the various resources from Catholic publishers. Invite someone to your session who has expertise or experience with the topic. As a permanent fix, with your catechetical leader, look for a co-catechist so that two of you will always minister together, each doing parts of the session that call forth your gifts.

CALMING MEDITATION ■ *God of Guidance, teach me your wisdom; be my lifeline.*

COMMITTED ACTION ■ Take time for prayer before preparing each session. Read, participate in adult formation sessions, and keep a list of those to whom you can go for support.

When I Want to Stay on Track with My Plans but Also Want to Be Open to the Spirit

The plans for our sessions are important; the sequence of sessions—with their content and learner participation—determined by catechetical publishers are fundamental to our faith learning.

At the same time, God is in the present moment. All types of things can happen suddenly and spontaneously in the lives of our learners, our parish, our world. When I was teaching in Las Vegas, it snowed one day in the city. Some children had seen snow in the mountains, but not falling snow outside their windows. Listening to the nudging of what was happening and to the Holy Spirit, I changed the prayer I had originally planned to a prayer of thanks for all the fascinating things God had created (falling snow, striped zebras, long-necked giraffes, color-changing chameleons, etc.).

CALMING MEDITATION ■ *God of Sensitivity, teach me the gift of discerning. Amid my preparedness and readiness, keep me also open and attentive to the present moment, to the needs, interests, and questions of my learners. Teach me to rely on the guidance of your Holy Spirit.*

COMMITTED ACTION ■ After prayerful preparation for each session, as you drive to and begin each session, be aware of the Holy Spirit's presence with you as you remember the title of Albert Cullum's classic book, *The Geranium on the Windowsill Just Died but Teacher You Went Right On*.

When I Don't Feel I Am Effective

When we think of the catechetical responsibility—to share the Catholic story; to be a witness of God's love, compassion, and faithfulness; and to connect our rich story to the everyday lives of the children/youth—we might ask ourselves: How can I ever do that?

The reality is this is not our work; it is God's work. If—or when—we think we can't do it, we are taking all the responsibility. We're forgetting that God will give us strength and guidance. God says to us, "You are the one I need. You are the one who will make a difference. I know you and I have chosen you. I will always be with you with gifts and support—more than you can imagine."

There's a saying that challenges and comforts us: "God doesn't call the qualified; God qualifies the called."

CALMING MEDITATION

And so, our Ever-Present God answers
all the questions and doubts
I might have,
saying encouragingly:
I can make all things well,
I will make all things well,
and I shall make all things well;
and you shall see yourself
that all manner of things shall be well.

(ADAPTED FROM JULIAN OF NORWICH, *REVELATIONS OF DIVINE LOVE*)

COMMITTED ACTION ■ Place sticky notes on your mirror, in your car, and in your catechist's manual with messages such as "I can do all things in God who strengthens me," "All shall be well," a favorite psalm verse, or another source of inspiration.

When I Feel Completely Overwhelmed

In today's world, there are often times when we feel totally swamped and exhausted. We have responded to the call to be a catechist. Yet, it is not the only role in our lives. Catechists are parents, grandparents, employees or employers, caregivers and volunteers at school, the parish, and local community organizations. In recent times, it feels as though each of these roles has tripled or quadrupled, and we wonder if we're doing a good job anywhere.

Sometimes the feeling of being overloaded comes from focusing on what the future holds. God invites us to live in the present moment, for that is where God is. Focusing on one moment, one task, one experience at a time—and knowing that God is with us in the moment—often helps us to live peacefully and vibrantly.

CALMING MEDITATION ■ Pray with the words of Psalm 46, omitting one word each time you pray the line:

Be still and know that I am God.
Be still and know that I am.
Be still and know that I.
Be still and know that.
Be still and know.
Be still and.
Be still.
Be.

COMMITTED ACTION ■ Reflect on one less thing. Is there something you're doing that might not need to be done anymore or that another person might be able to do (providing them the chance to serve and give)?

When Children/Youth Speak Unkindly To Each Other

There are times our learners are not their most kind and caring selves. This can lead to hurtful teasing or bullying. Faith formation is an invitation for people of all ages to live a life of virtue, integrity, and goodness. We have the power of being a countersign, a witness, a guide.

Here are three ways of "teaching" kindness: 1) Be sure all your words and actions are kind, respectful, and considerate. 2) At the beginning of the year, invite your learners to set the guidelines for your gatherings. Be sure they include only kind words and actions toward others. 3) Never let an instance of unkindness or bullying happen without comment and learning from it (individually or with the whole group).

CALMING MEDITATION ■ Loving-kindness meditation is a prayer of blessing for others, for deepening their gifts of compassion and kindness, the gifts and fruits of the Holy Spirit within them. As you call to mind each of your learners, repeatedly pray:

May you be held in God's loving kindness.
May you be filled with loving kindness.
May you grow in gentleness and goodness.
May God's peace and love surround you
as you share them with others.

COMMITTED ACTION ■ Visit the Random Acts of Kindness Foundation (https://randomactsofkindness.org/) for free educational and community ideas, guidance, and other resources.

When I Feel Like Something Is Missing

My one-year-old great-niece was enjoying lunch so much that after each spoonful, she said, "More, more!" Is there something about our catechetical process that inspires the call for "more, more!"?

The "more, more!" is that our faith touches all of life. What should we be doing in every gathering time? Touching the head, the heart, and the hands. Faith formation is about knowing something, being something, doing something.

Sometimes, because of time, we might stop with the head. We share all the facts and beliefs. They are important! Yet, even in knowing all that is needed, the real questions are: What difference does it make? Who am I? What am I called to do?

In touching the heart, we experience that we are called to be friends with God, that God calls us to an intimate friendship—which touches who I am and all I'm called to be and do. In touching the head and heart, formation and life overflow to our hands: our call to do something. To be disciples is to do what Jesus did, what Jesus would do today in our world.

CALMING MEDITATION ■ *God of All Life, guide me as your message molds our heads, our hearts, and our hands—to know you, to love you, to be your presence in our world.*

COMMITTED ACTION ■ Check your plans for next week. How are you touching heads, hearts, and hands?

When I Wonder: Does Anyone Really Care?

Planning time and our weekly faith formation sessions involve a great deal of time, energy, faith, and love. At times we wonder: Does anyone really know what this entails? Does anyone really understand and appreciate the many things we do to make learning a little more attractive, enjoyable, and meaningful?

Paul prays, "Blessed be the God and Father of our Lord Jesus Christ, the Father of compassion and God of all encouragement..." (2 Corinthians 1:3). God not only understands but reassures us. Even when others do not seem to notice or appreciate all we do as catechists, God does.

CALMING MEDITATION ■ Breath is all-important! We breathe in to provide our bodies with oxygen; we breathe out to get rid of carbon dioxide. So, too, we pray, remembering that the Holy Spirit is often called the breath of God.

Breathe in God's love; breathe out insecurity.
Breathe in God's reassurance; breathe out discouragement.
Breathe in God's vision; breathe out negativity.
Breathe in God's support; breathe out aloneness.
Breathe in God's joy; breathe out unhappiness.
Breathe in God's peace; breathe out tension or anxiety.

COMMITTED ACTION ■ Save thank-you notes that you receive from your learners or their parents. Keep a list of thank yous and compliments you receive. On your discouraging days, reread them, reflecting on how God has supported you in your ministry of being God's face to so many.

When One of my Learners Has Experienced a Major Loss, such as the Death of a Parent

This is certainly a situation which we hope we never have to face, but the reality is that we probably will. While each child/youth will be affected differently depending on their age, personal characteristics, family situation, and previous experiences, one thing is certain: not acknowledging grief can be detrimental.

Be attentive, kind, and open to listening. Know that some children may have a difficult time expressing their feelings or may not be ready to talk. When they have questions you're not sure of, refer them to adults who can answer them. Remember that grief often lasts for a very long time.

Throughout your year's themes, whenever possible, talk about the Paschal Mystery—which we live all the time with Jesus: suffering, death (in all kinds of ways), and new life.

CALMING MEDITATION ■ *Consoling God, your Son Jesus wept at the death of his friend Lazarus. Help me, because of my own losses, to deepen my understanding and compassion for others. Help me to find the words—and ways of presence—when my learners are experiencing the death of a loved one.*

COMMITTED ACTION ■ Encourage your parish to host a helpful library of books, articles, and other resources that talk about the grief of children as well as books about death written for children. Become aware of local and national organizations that minister to grieving children/youth and their families.

When I Am Unsure of All the Answers

A bishop new to his diocese visited the oldest priest in the diocese, asking, "What has helped you to stay faithful in ministry for so many years?" Without hesitation, the older priest replied, "Well...I knew someone who knew someone who knew someone who knew someone who knew someone who knew someone who knew someone who knew Jesus."

Who you are is most important. Your relationship with Jesus is most important. Because you know Jesus, you will make a difference in the lives of your young people. As we pass on the faith, more is caught than taught.

It's not that "knowing our faith" isn't extremely important; we always have an imperative responsibility to continue our learning and growing. At the same time, all the preparation and study in the world will never give us all the answers to every question (and that's exciting, for there is always more to learn). It's all right to say, "I'm not sure, but I'll find out during the week and we'll talk more about it next week." Encourage your learners, too, to do research, to talk to their parents and grandparents to find the answer.

CALMING MEDITATION ■ *God of Mystery, open my eyes, my ears, and my heart to learn more deeply, to teach more earnestly.*

COMMITTED ACTION ■ Enroll in a class, participate in a parish or diocesan workshop, or read a book to deepen your understanding of the faith.

When There's So Much to Share

At times, most catechists—for various reasons—have the feeling that the ministry of catechist is an impossible undertaking. Often one reason is being overwhelmed by the amount of information we have to share in a short time.

As committed, caring catechists, it's natural that we want to share so much about the rich tradition and gift of our faith. Yet, the learning and living of our faith, our relationship with God, is a lifelong endeavor. We don't have to present, explore, and reflect on everything about our faith in one year!

Diocesan guidelines and the composition of our catechetical texts provide and guide a systematic, comprehensive, and age-appropriate learning experience. Many texts today employ a spiral structure to the teaching of our Catholic faith: core teachings of our faith are revisited in greater depth at each age level.

CALMING MEDITATION ■ In the midst of feeling that the task is larger than we are, follow the advice of the spiritual writer Henri Nouwen, who wrote: "We can use the Lord's Prayer, the Jesus Prayer, the name of Jesus, or any word that reminds us of God's love and put it in the center of our inner room, like a candle in a dark space."

COMMITTED ACTION ■ Take time to peruse the Scope and Sequence charts of the catechetical series you are using as well as the charts from your diocesan catechetical office. Notice that you don't have to do it all!

When I Think That Nothing Got Accomplished

Sometimes after a session, we feel that all we did was struggle for their attention and/or attend to problems. "Some days are like that," remarks Alexander in Judith Viorst's book *Alexander and the Terrible, Horrible, No Good, Very Bad Day*.

Perhaps the question is: How did we respond? Often the things we do, and how we do them, teach a great deal! Our challenge is—in the midst of these "some days"—to remain peacefully centered in God, to be kind and considerate as well as calling the young people to the "more, more" of respectful behavior and participation.

After some sessions, we might feel that the content of the session plan didn't get across; amid all the distractions, there wasn't sufficient time to explore it. Yet, what did happen? How did we respond? Did our faithfulness to God, our respect for each person, our desire for the best for each learner, our peace-filled demeanor, our commitment to learning and growing in our faith journey "teach" the children or youth?

CALMING MEDITATION ■ Take time for Centering Prayer, especially before your sessions: a time of quiet without words, time to experience the loving presence and strength of God that will then keep you peacefully centered in God amid distractions and interruptions.

COMMITTED ACTION ■ When you're away from these "some days" for a little bit of time, reflect—and give thanks—for all the blessings that did happen on these days.

When I Feel I'm in a Slump

Often in the middle of the year, we might feel like we're in a rut. We're back to "ordinary time," and everything seems kind of boring.

One human tendency is to see things as a series of steps to get through: there's an exciting beginning, but then we're always waiting to reach the end. Hence, the middle can be tedious and tiresome. What if we saw things as God does: everything is a new beginning, and this present moment is spectacular and filled with possibilities?

The middle can be a time of assessment, bringing to mind all the good things that are happening: What is my goal as a catechist; how has my prayer changed; what have the children responded to most enthusiastically?

The middle can be a time of change and new approaches: Is there a new way to pray during our sessions; a new activity; an opportunity to invite a guest speaker; unique ways to invite the learners to take responsibility within our sessions?

CALMING MEDITATION ■ *God of the Middle Times, open my imagination, my creativity, and my senses to all the new promises lurking in every corner of my world, especially in the learning times with my young people and their families.*

COMMITTED ACTION ■ Do one thing differently within your sessions: change the seating and environment; use more music, poetry, and drama; ask more "What if" questions; use technology for learning and prayer.

When I Feel Disappointed That a Session Did Not Go Well

We always have expectations and hopes. At times we experience disappointment because things don't go as we planned. There are challenges and gifts in that.

Challenges: Disappointment could lead us to discouragement and the desire to give up, feeling it's not worthwhile.

Gifts: Disappointment can encourage us to reflect, examine, and try new things. It can help us realize it was only one time, giving us the inspiration to begin again. An anonymous quote reminds us: "One cannot feel true disappointment until the very end, and even then, it is only another beginning."

Sometimes, too, what we might think was a failed session touched our learners in ways we're not aware of! Their response is not always ours.

And, certainly, our disappointment reminds us it's not our work; our success is in God. "Those who wait for the Lord shall renew their strength, they shall mount up with wings like eagles, they shall run and not be weary, they shall walk and not faint" (Isaiah 40:31).

CALMING MEDITATION ■ *Strengthening God, you are with me in the disappointments. Awaken in me, once again, my passion and commitment for your work and my learners. Give me your courage and enthusiasm.*

COMMITTED ACTION ■ Take a few minutes after each session to reflect with God on how things went. Journal about three things that went well. Decide on how you can enhance and expand them in the sessions to come.

When I Wonder If My Suggestions for At-Home Activities Are Meaningful

Your ministry is not just for the young people but for their entire families. A few reminders and suggestions:

- Don't call it "homework." Faith formation is very different from everyday school.
- Involve the parents/families. For instance, the children can interview their parents, asking questions such as "When do you pray? Whom do you pray to? Why do you pray?" when the session is on prayer. Families can be invited to watch a specific TV show and be given questions to analyze the show (or the commercials) according to Gospel values, Jesus' lifestyle, or a specific theme currently being studied.
- Don't feel you have to invent new ideas; rely on the family suggestions in your manual. Tweak them for your families.

CALMING MEDITATION ■ *God who called us as families, show me how to support a family faith that is alive, compassionate, joyful, tangible, and practical.*

COMMITTED ACTION ■ Have a sounding board of a few parents (or involve all the parents on a rotating basis). Ask for their evaluations of past activities and/or recommendations for future ones.

When a Session Went Really Well

Our previous meditations were about the challenging, demanding times; we need to rely on our God during these tough times. We can also go to God in thanksgiving during all the positive times!

There might be many more of these positive times, but, for some reason, we have a tendency to highlight and concentrate on the problematic ones. The next few meditations will urge us to pay attention to, be grateful for, and build on the successful and graced times.

How do we judge if our sessions have gone really well? Many times, we might have a satisfying feeling about all that happened. At times, our learners might remark about what they learned or about how they enjoyed a particular activity. At times, do we view our sessions through God's eyes? What would be all the advantageous things that God saw? Which of your words echoed the words of Jesus in the Gospels? How did prayer provide a chance for everyone to be one with God?

CALMING MEDITATION ■ *God of Generous Giving, I have so much to be grateful for. Thank you, thank you! Help me to be more aware of all the good that happens, all that surrounds my learners and myself, as you guide and protect us.*

COMMITTED ACTION ■ At the conclusion of each catechetical session, write down (at the end of your session plans), three things, people, or happenings for which you are grateful.

When I Saw a Child/Youth Do Something We Talked About

Sometimes we wonder if things are making sense, if anything is touching the hearts and the lives of our learners. Perhaps we are looking for the magnificent, the marvelous, a world-changing action. Yet, most of our lives—most of the lives of our learners—are lived in the everyday, the simple, the routine, the ordinary.

When we pay attention to the commonplace and the familiar, we often discover in the actions of our learners all that they are absorbing about living the life of discipleship: responding with respect, caring about someone who is lonely, acting with courtesy, reaching out to someone who has been treated unjustly, taking responsibility without being asked, apologizing and forgiving, praying with sincerity, helping without expecting a reward, volunteering for ministry, and so on.

CALMING MEDITATION ■ *God of Watchfulness, you watch and see all the goodness in your world, especially the kindness and generosity of my learners. With gratitude in my heart, lead me to carefully notice all their loving actions.*

COMMITTED ACTION ■ Think about what you think about; watch what you look for. "Whatever is true, whatever is honorable, whatever is just, whatever is pure, whatever is pleasing, whatever is commendable, if there is any excellence and if there is anything worthy of praise, think about these things" (Philippians 4:8). Think about and watch for all the good that your learners are doing.

When I Met God in an Unexpected Way

Have you ever planned a session (which you thought was going to be very successful) or planned a prayer time (which you felt was effectively connecting the session's theme to the everyday experiences of your learners and providing the atmosphere for an encounter with God) and found that something unexpected happened? (You're not sure you can even put it into words.)

It might have been a response from a child; a feeling of peace and community within your group; an awareness of the Holy Spirit's guidance; a comment from another catechist just before the session.

You were expecting to experience God because of all your planning; yet God was there in an unexpected word, from an unexpected person, in an unexpected way. The surprising gifts of God!

CALMING MEDITATION ■ *Lectio divina* is a prayer form that at times brings unexpected words from God. At least once a week, read a short passage from Scripture. Listen—not to learn the meaning of the whole text, but listen to the Spirit, listen for a word or phrase that grabs your attention: What is it saying to you today, this moment? Talk to, listen to, rest in God. Because of that word, what action is God calling you to take?

COMMITTED ACTION ■ Try not to program God, placing your expectations on God and how God works. Be open: watch and listen carefully for the multiple, constant, marvelous ways God surrounds you.

When I Was Able to Connect with a Parent

Sometimes we can find ourselves in a conversation (or in our own thoughts) in which we easily blame parents for all the things we think they are doing incorrectly. Perhaps, at times, they do need nudging and reminders, yet how often do we put ourselves in their shoes, trying to understand their multiple tasks and responsibilities? How often do we look for all the good, affirming, and effective things they do, day in and day out?

When we get to know the interests and needs of the parents of our learners, when we take time to compliment and praise them, we are showing them the loving face of God. Think about the parents who have responded to you, connected with you, been grateful to you because of your affirmation of them.

CALMING MEDITATION ■ *Parenting God, bless the parents of my learners; keep them always in your care. Help me, with your grace, to be a support and grateful presence for each of them. Help us to work together so that the young people will grow in truth and love within the embrace of their homes and my catechetical sessions.*

COMMITTED ACTION ■ Remember and reach out during the events and happenings in the lives of the parents of your learners, such as the death of a parent, a new baby, loss of a job, a significant anniversary. Find every possible way to affirm and support them in their daily lives.